# Do You Really Want a Hamster?

Bridget Heos • Illustrated by Katya Longhi

amicus
illustrated

amicus
illustrated

Amicus Illustrated is published by Amicus
P.O. Box 1329, Mankato, MN 56002
www.amicuspublishing.us

Library of Congress Cataloging-in-Publication Data
Heos, Bridget.
 Do you really want a hamster? / by Bridget Heos ; illustrated by
Katya Longhi.
     pages cm. — (Do you really want— ?)
 Includes bibliographical references.
 Summary: "Mischievous hamsters (and the narrator) teach a young boy
the responsibility—and the joys—of owning a hamster. Includes 'Is this pet
right for me?' quiz"—Provided by publisher.
 ISBN 978-1-60753-206-4 (library binding) — ISBN 978-1-60753-398-6 (ebook)
 1. Hamsters as pets—Juvenile literature. I. Longhi, Katya, illustrator. II. Title.
 SF459.H3H46 2014
 636.935'6—dc23
                        2012035932

Editor: Rebecca Glaser
Designer: The Design Lab

Printed in the United States of America at Corporate Graphics
in North Mankato, Minnesota.

Date 1/2014  PO 1190

10 9 8 7 6 5 4 3 2

# About the Author

Bridget Heos is the author of more than
40 books for children and teens, including
*What to Expect When You're Expecting Larvae*
(2011, Lerner). She lives in Kansas City with
husband Justin, sons Johnny, Richie, and
J.J., plus a dog, cat, and Guinea pig.
You can visit her online at
www.authorbridgetheos.com.

# About the Illustrator

Katya Longhi was born in southern Italy.
She studied illustration at the Nemo NT
Academy of Digital Arts in Florence. She loves
to create dream worlds with horses, flying
dogs, and princesses in her illustrations.
She currently lives in northern Italy
with her Prince Charming.

So you say you want a hamster. You really, really want a hamster. **But do you *really* want a hamster?**

If you have a hamster, you'll need to give him fresh water and feed him every day.

If you don't…

… he'll be starving,
and thirsty,
and sad.

And don't feed him the same thing over and over. Besides pellets and seeds, feed him fresh vegetables, fruit, and an occasional treat.

Use the treats to train your hamster.
**If you don't train him…**

. . . he'll run away when
you try to hold him.

Train your hamster in the evening, when he wakes up. (Hamsters sleep during the day. They are nocturnal.) Hold your hand in the cage. Talk softly. Hold a treat in your hand. At first, he'll only eat the treat.

After a while…

. . . he might climb onto your hand.

Then he might stay
there for a while.

Now you can gently lift him out of the cage using two hands. Careful not to drop him! And don't squeeze him. Put him down if he is scared.

If he's not...

. . . maybe he'd like to do something fun. Like run through a maze.

Or roll in a ball.

Don't leave your hamster
unsupervised outside his cage.

If you do…

. . . he could get lost! And a house
is a dangerous place for a hamster.

You'll need a cozy (but high security) hamster cage. Hamsters are also brilliant escape artists.

Hamsters want everything in its place. The cage should be big enough so that each corner can be its own room: Dining room. Bedroom. Bathroom. Personal Gym.

It doesn't have to be *that* fancy. More like this: A corner for food and water, a place to sleep and hide, an exercise area—containing a wheel or tunnels, and a corner for going potty. For bedding, use wood chips.

Clean the bathroom area daily
and the whole cage weekly.

Otherwise...

Speaking of having
two hamsters . . .
should you or
shouldn't you?

It depends. Some types of dwarf hamsters like sharing a cage.

But keep an eye on them. If they fight, they may need to be separated. Other hamsters can't live together at all. Golden hamsters and Chinese dwarf hamsters should live alone.

Whether you have one or two, hamsters are fun playmates. Even when they're in their cage, you can cheer them on.

So if you're willing to feed, water, play with, and clean his cage, then maybe you really do want a hamster.

Now I have a question for the hamster.
You say you want a person.
You really, really want a person.
**But do you *really* want a person?**

# QUIZ

## Is this the right pet for me?

Should you get a hamster? Take this quiz to find out. (Be sure to talk to breeders, rescue groups, or pet store workers, too!)

1. Do you have a quiet spot in your house for a cage?
2. Do you have the time and patience to tame an animal?
3. Do you like tiny animals, and can you be very calm and careful with them?
4. Can you wait until evening to play with your animal?

## If you answered . . .

a. NO TO ONE OR FOUR, a rodent that's active during the day, such as a gerbil, Guinea pig, or rat, may be a better fit.
b. NO TO TWO, an animal that stays in its cage, such as a finch, may be better.
c. NO TO THREE, you may like a larger animal, such as a dog or cat.
d. YES TO ALL FOUR QUESTIONS, a hamster might be the right pet for you!

# Websites

AAHA Healthy Pets Kids Klub
*http://www.healthypet.com/KidsKlub/Default.aspx*
This site, sponsored by the American Animal Hospital Association, features fun facts, coloring sheets, games, and tips on animal care.

ASPCA Kids
*http://www.aspca.org/aspcakids.aspx*
The American Society for the Prevention of Cruelty to Animals provides games, photos, and videos that demonstrate pet care, plus information on careers working with animals.

Hamster Care and Behavior Tips:
The Humane Society of the United States
*http://www.humanesociety.org/animals/hamsters/tips/ hamster_tips.html*
The Humane Society has advice on choosing a hamster cage, bringing a hamster home, and feeding.

Tama and Friends visit Petfinder.com
*http://www.petfinder.com/tama//index.html*
The kids' section of Petfinder.com offers games, pet tips, pet listings, and a section for parents.

# Read More

Gaines, Ann Graham. *Top 10 Small Mammals for Kids*. Enslow Elementary, 2009.

Johnson, Jinny. *Hamsters and Gerbils*. Get to Know Your Pet. Smart Apple Media, 2009.

Niven, Felicia Lowenstein. *Learning to Care for Small Mammals*. Beginning Pet Care with American Humane. Bailey Books, 2011.

Smalley, Carol Parenzan. *Care for a Pet Hamster*. How to Convince Your Parents You Can—Mitchell Lane Publishers, 2010.

Zobel, Derek. *Caring for Your Hamster*. Bellwether Media, 2011.